THE GOLDEN COCKEREL

THE YOUNG READER'S GUIDES TO MUSIC

THE GOLDEN COCKEREL

Three Stories of Magic and Witchcraft from Russian Opera

BY

ENID GIBSON

Illustrated by

PRUDENCE THEOBALDS

NEW YORK
HENRY Z. WALCK, INCORPORATED
1963

PRINTED IN GREAT BRITAIN

INTRODUCTION

THE THREE TALES in this book are from Russian operas. An opera is a story in words and music, in which the characters sing their parts instead of speaking them as they do in a play. You can enjoy the stories perfectly well even if you never hear the music. But really the music is every bit as important as the words, and if you get a chance to hear any of these operas you will find them even more exciting.

The Russians have always been very fond of stories of fairies, witches, and wizards, and Russian composers have liked setting them to music. The witch Baba Yaga, for instance, comes in Mussorgsky's *Pictures at an Exhibition,* and the magician Kaschchei the Deathless in Stravinsky's *The Firebird.* All Tchaikovsky's ballets, too are about witchcraft and magic.

There are many Russian operas with fairy-tale stories, but these three are probably the best to start off with. I think you will enjoy them.

CONTENTS

RUSLAN AND LUDMILLA

A GREAT many years ago, King Svetozar reigned in the city of Kiev, in Russia. He had a daughter called Ludmilla, who was so beautiful and good that princes came from all over the world to ask for her hand in marriage. But Ludmilla refused them all, until only three were left: Prince Ratmir, who came from a southern land; Farlaf, a bully and a coward; and Ruslan, the bravest of all knights.

At last Ludmilla chose Ruslan to be her bridegroom, and King Svetozar gave a great feast to celebrate their betrothal. All the guests agreed that Ruslan and Ludmilla were the handsomest couple they had ever seen, and wished them every possible joy and happiness in their life together.

But not Farlaf: *he* hated Ruslan for being brave and fortunate. Young Ratmir, the other suitor, was not jealous. He was a good-natured prince and wanted Ludmilla to be happy above all.

☆ *1* ☆

King Svetozar headed the table at the feast, with his daughter Ludmilla on his right and Ruslan on his left; beyond them sat Farlaf, Ratmir, and other honoured guests. The table was

The minstrel sings

crammed with golden dishes of food and goblets of wine. And all the time there was music and singing and story-telling.

Svetozar's own minstrel knew more tunes and ballads than anyone. At the height of the banquet he sang a song that he had made up specially for the occasion. This minstrel was a wise man, and could see into the future. He struck up a slow tune on his harp and began to sing rather sadly. His words warned the young couple to expect danger, which often comes when it is least expected. The courtiers and guests were puzzled. Why should the minstrel choose to sing such a sad song on that day of all days? At least he might have waited until the feast was over! Only Farlaf was glad to hear the minstrel's warning. 'Perhaps Ruslan will be killed,' he thought, 'and then I can marry Ludmilla after all!'

The King was angry. 'What dismal croaking is this?' he cried. 'Give us a merry song!' So the minstrel began a more cheerful verse this time. 'In the darkest hours hope shines like a star and leads the way to happiness,' he sang. The guests liked this better, and laughter and chat began to rise once more from the long tables. Ludmilla turned to Ratmir and Farlaf and asked them not to be angry with her for choosing another man for her husband. She felt sure they would both find better brides for themselves in their own countries.

Then King Svetozar gave his blessing to his daughter and Ruslan; the party was at its most cheerful. Suddenly there was a hideous clap of thunder, and the great hall was plunged into darkness! There was a moment of panic. Then the smoking torches flared up again, and the guests stared at one another in amazement. But King Svetozar gave a cry of dismay: in that second of darkness Ludmilla had disappeared from her place beside him! He sent servants running to look for her, but although they searched in every corner of the palace there was no trace of the princess. Her father was in despair. He was horribly afraid that she had been spirited away by some evil spell. In his anguish he promised to give her in marriage to whichever of her suitors succeeded in finding her and bringing her back safe. Although Ruslan was her chosen bridegroom, he must take his chance with the rest.

The three young men lost no time. Farlaf was delighted to be given another opportunity to win Ludmilla after all. Ratmir wanted to save her from harm. And Ruslan was impatient to

☆ 3 ☆

seek her out wherever she might be hidden in the whole wide world.

☆   ☆   ☆

They rode out together from the palace. Ruslan soon got ahead, for his horse was the swiftest and he rode the hardest. He rode on and on for many days, and at length came to a dark cave in a hillside. An old man came out and called to him: 'Welcome, Ruslan; I have been expecting you.' 'Who are you?' asked Ruslan, 'and how did you know my name?'

'Ah,' said the old man, 'I also know that Ludmilla has been stolen away by the Black Dwarf, who is a powerful magician and very wicked. But you will conquer him and rescue Ludmilla. As to me,' he continued sadly, 'I come from Finland, where I was once a happy boy, looking after cattle. I fell in love with a beautiful girl called Naina. She just laughed at me. So, going to the Wise Men who live in my country, I studied with them for many years. At last I became as wise as they, and thought I could now win Naina's love. But I had learned so much that I discovered her secret: Naina too was a clever magician. She had made herself young and beautiful by her spells, but really she was an old, ugly, wicked witch! I ran away from her in horror, and ever since then she has hated me for discovering her secret. That is why I hide in this dark cave. She will hate you too, Ruslan, when she knows you are my friend.'

'I am not afraid of any witch!' Ruslan cried defiantly.

'Good,' said the old Finn; 'I knew you were brave and strong. Now you must ride on to the Land of Midnight, far to the north, where the Black Dwarf's castle is. Nobody has ever been able to get in without his consent, but you must. Ludmilla is there. Only don't forget the witch, Naina.'

Ruslan meets the old Finn

Ruslan thanked the Finn for his advice and set off for the far north. The journey was long and dangerous, and he often had to fight his way through enemies. In one of these fights his horse was killed, and in another his sword was broken.

At last he found himself in the most terrifying place he had ever seen. It was a battlefield, shrouded in mist. No trees or grass or flowers grew there; only the bones of dead soldiers and their rusty, splintered armour lay about the ground.

Sadly Ruslan wondered what brave men had fought there. He picked up some of the rusty swords, but they were all too small and light for him. Suddenly a thunderous voice called out: 'Do not disturb the bones of men who died in battle!' The mist lifted a little, and Ruslan saw an enormous head in a knight's helmet. It had no body, but stood on its neck in the middle of the field.

Ruslan was terrified. A head without a body—which could speak! As he stared at it the head spoke again: 'Leave the bones and armour alone. I am here to guard them, and if you stay I will kill you!' It opened its huge mouth wide and blew, making a hot wind howl across the battlefield. This made Ruslan angry. He struck the head with his spear so hard that it rocked to and fro on its stump of neck. As it did so

Ruslan saw something shiny on the ground beneath it—something that looked like a sword. He bent down and snatched it as quick as a flash. It *was* a long, heavy sword, and although the head groaned pitifully at losing its treasure, Ruslan fastened it in his belt.

Then the head told Ruslan its story. 'I used to live with my only brother,' it said; 'I, the giant, and my brother the Black Dwarf.' 'The Black Dwarf? He is your brother?' asked Ruslan eagerly. 'Yes, but he hates me,' replied the head. 'I won this magic sword in battle, you see. It is the only sword that can cut off my brother's long beard, and all his magic power lies in that beard. I wouldn't give up the sword, but he was more cunning than I. He suggested that the first of us to hear voices speaking from the earth should keep the sword. Like a fool, I lay down with my ear to the ground, and he struck off my head. Then he brought me here and put the sword beneath my neck, thinking it would be safe. Now *you* must find the Black Dwarf, my brother, and cut off his magic beard; then I shall be revenged.'

'I will, I will,' cried Ruslan, drawing the sword from his belt and brandishing it above his head as if it had been no more than a stick.

☆　　☆　　☆

Ludmilla's other suitors, Ratmir and Farlaf, were still searching for her. But Farlaf was beginning to get tired of all the dangers he met. He was thinking longingly of his comfortable castle when he met a hideous old woman. Farlaf at once knew her to be a witch. 'Oh, please don't put a curse on me!' he stammered. Now the old woman was Naina, the witch who was the Finn's enemy. 'Don't be afraid,' she cackled. 'Go home and wait for me there. *I* will find Ludmilla for you.' Farlaf was delighted with this friendly witch, and galloped home as fast as his horse could carry him.

Ratmir had many adventures too, though none so dangerous as Ruslan's. He got very tired, riding through the land. At last he came to a splendid palace, with lots of beautiful girls to welcome him. They gave him delicious food, and sang and danced for him so entrancingly that Ratmir began to forget all about his search for Ludmilla. This palace was the witch Naina's and the girls were her slaves. They bewitched the travellers who came there, making them forget all their past lives. So Ratmir lay on a soft couch and listened to the magic music, and thought no longer of Ludmilla or Ruslan, nor even of his own homeland far away in the south.

Soon Ruslan too arrived at this enchanted palace. He thought perhaps it was the Black Dwarf's. Immediately the music and the dancing began to bewitch him as well. He sat beside his friend Ratmir on the couch and thought he would like to stay there for ever.

How long they would have stayed there nobody can tell. But fortunately Ruslan had a friend who kept a better watch for him than he did for himself: the old Finn! Suddenly he was there, pushing his way through the slave girls, who ran about the hall in terror. His eyes flashed angrily when he saw Ruslan lolling back among silk cushions. The music ceased. Ruslan jumped to his feet and quickly picked up his sword. He realized that he had been under a spell. With a wave of his magic staff, the Finn turned Naina's palace into a wild forest.

'This is no way to find Ludmilla,' the old man said to Ruslan and Ratmir. 'Who will rescue her if you fall into the first trap

The Finn waved his magic staff

the witch sets for you? You must hurry to the Black Dwarf's castle as fast as you can!' Ashamed at having been tricked so easily, Ruslan and Ratmir promised not to forget their quest again, and started on the last stage of their search together.

☆   ☆   ☆

All this time Ludmilla had been kept a prisoner by the wicked Black Dwarf at his castle in the Land of Midnight. She was in the garden, watched over by sprites, and nymphs, and elves. They tried to persuade her to marry their master. They brought her jewels and lovely dresses. A table covered with the most delicious fruit and sweets was made to rise up out of the ground before her eyes. 'You will *never* see Ruslan again!' the sprites told her. 'But if you marry the Black Dwarf you will have these things every day'.

But Ludmilla turned away indignantly. 'I am Svetozar's daughter, a princess of Kiev,' she said proudly. 'I am not to be bribed. I will marry no one but Ruslan.' At last she fell asleep, weeping for Ruslan, and the nymphs sang a lullaby.

Soon the Black Dwarf himself appeared. A long procession came out of the castle into the garden where Ludmilla lay. It was led by musicians, then came servants and pages in brightly-coloured clothes, and a leaping crowd of dancers. At last the noise of drums and cymbals woke Ludmilla from her sleep. She sat up and saw several small black boys, one behind the other, carrying cushions on which lay what looked like long, black hair. This was the Black Dwarf's beard! He sat down on a great ebony throne, while the boys draped his beard over the steps in front of him. The beard, which, you remember, held all his magic powers, was the most impressive thing about the Black Dwarf, for he was very short and extremely ugly. He beckoned Ludmilla to sit beside him. She shook her head, but some of the slaves dragged her to a stool at his side.

Then the Black Dwarf raised his gnarled hand and the dancers began: first with a Turkish dance, then with an Arab dance, a Tartar dance, and finally a Caucasian dance. Ludmilla was too weary and unhappy to enjoy it, though the dancers were clever and beautiful. She was glad when a loud trumpet-call broke up the entertainment.

The trumpet sounded again, and the slaves and nymphs crowded towards the castle gates to see who it could be. But they quickly scattered with cries of fear, for it was Ruslan, the bravest of all knights, holding his great sword in his hand!

Instantly the cunning Dwarf cast a spell over Ludmilla, so that she fell into a deep sleep. Then he picked up his club and rushed to meet Ruslan. But Ruslan remembered what the strange head on the battlefield had told him: he quickly seized the Black Dwarf's beard and cut it off with one stroke of the magic sword. After that the Dwarf was no longer a magician but only an ordinary man, and in a few moments he was dead at Ruslan's hands. Triumphantly, Ruslan wound the long beard round his helmet. The Dwarf's slaves knelt before him as he did so, for they were bound to serve whoever wore the beard. Followed by Ratmir, now his loyal friend, Ruslan ran joyously to where Ludmilla lay. Imagine his grief when he found that he could not wake her from her enchanted sleep! The Black Dwarf's spell was still too strong for them, although he was dead. Angrily Ruslan ordered the slaves to prepare a litter for the princess. 'We will carry her back to her own country,' he cried. 'The cleverest doctors there will surely be able to wake her!' The slaves did their new master's bidding, and soon they all set out on the long road back to the city of Kiev.

But there were further troubles in store: Naina the witch was still determined to capture Ludmilla and marry her to Farlaf. One night during the long journey southwards, the wicked witch stole the princess away once more while Ruslan and Ratmir lay sleeping.

When Ruslan awoke he was nearly mad with rage and despair. He rode off at once to begin his search all over again. Ratmir was so bewildered he did not know what to do. 'Poor Ruslan,' he sighed; 'poor Ludmilla. What am I to do? If only the Finn were here to help us!'

Immediately a voice spoke at his elbow. 'Don't be afraid,' it said. 'Here I am!' And there stood the good Finn, holding in his hand a beautiful ring.

Ratmir was overjoyed. 'What must we do to save Ludmilla?' he asked eagerly. 'This is Naina's last spell,' explained the Finn. 'If it fails, she cannot harm any of you again. Take this magic ring to Kiev. You will meet Ruslan on the way, and Ludmilla is already back at the palace. Tell Ruslan the ring will awaken her, and they will be happy for evermore.'

Ratmir did exactly as he was told. He rode on towards Kiev, and met Ruslan wandering despairingly across the wide plain. But when Ruslan heard the Finn's message and saw the ring, he recovered his spirits. Together Ruslan and Ratmir hurried to Kiev and to King Svetozar's castle.

Ratmir and the magic ring

In the meantime Farlaf had brought Ludmilla in her litter to the King, with the story that *he* had rescued her from the Black Dwarf. The King was so glad to see his daughter again that he greeted Farlaf like a son; in any case he had no reason to doubt his word. But when he found he could not wake Ludmilla, he was angry. 'I promised my daughter to the one who would bring her back to me,' he said to Farlaf, 'but I want her alive and laughing, as she used to be! Wake her, knight!'

The frightened Farlaf did his best, but he could not break the spell. Svetozar, in his bitter disappointment, would have thrown Farlaf into prison if Ruslan had not come striding into the hall at that moment.

'Ruslan—at last *you* are here!' cried the King. 'You have always loved my daughter best: surely *you* can save her?'

Ruslan smiled. He went towards the sleeping girl and held out the Finn's beautiful ring. And immediately Ludmilla's eyelids began to flutter, the colour crept back into her face, and she awoke to find herself in her father's palace once more— with Ruslan beside her. It would have been difficult to say who was happiest: she, or her faithful Ruslan, or her father, or the gentle Ratmir and the watching courtiers.

Ruslan and Ludmilla were married the next day, and lived happily ever after. Ratmir went back to his own warm country and married a girl he had known since he was a child. The Finn was the guest of honour at Ruslan's wedding and became a great friend of King Svetozar's.

As for Farlaf, he crept away out of the castle as soon as Ruslan appeared with the ring, and neither he, nor Naina, were ever heard of again.

THE MUSIC

RUSLAN AND LUDMILLA was the first really Russian opera. Up to 1842, when it was put on at St. Petersburg (now Leningrad), the operas performed in Russia were nearly all Italian.

Glinka (1804-57), the composer of *Ruslan*, had been fond of his native Russian folk-songs since childhood, and he determined to compose Russian operas. In *Ruslan and Ludmilla*, his second opera, he found the true Russian style he had been looking for. Nearly all other Russian composers have been influenced by it, and so Glinka is often called 'the father of Russian music.'

He took the story from a long poem by Pushkin, a friend of his, and one of the greatest of Russian poets. The whole opera is seldom performed, but you can hear it on records, and some of it is played at concerts—especially the Overture. This contains the tune of the final chorus of rejoicing; and the rousing tune Ruslan sings while he is searching for a sword on the battlefield. There is also a fascinating song which Farlaf sings after the witch has told him to go and wait at home while she finds Ludmilla for him. It makes a good concert aria for a deep bass singer. The music fairly bubbles over with delight— Farlaf is so relieved at not having to do any fighting!

The other pieces from *Ruslan and Ludmilla* which you can sometimes hear separately are:

1. The beautiful chorus sung by Naina's spirits to bewitch Ratmir.

2. A suite of magic dances from the same scene.

3. The march that accompanies the Black Dwarf's appearance in his castle garden, with the pages carrying his beard on cushions; and

4. The oriental dances—Turkish, Arab, Tartar and Caucasian—that the Black Dwarf's slaves perform to entertain him and Ludmilla.

THE GOLDEN COCKEREL

ONE DAY, King Dodon and all his nobles were' sitting in the great palace council-chamber. It was very hot. The sentries by the staircase had gone to sleep.

The old King began to speak. He was worried, he said. Things were better in the good old days. When he was a young man *he* led out his army and invaded his enemies' territories, but now—why, his enemies invaded *his* country. 'It isn't fair,' he grumbled; 'I never know where to expect them. If I think they're going to attack in the north, they come from the south! What on earth are we to do?'

The King's eldest son jumped to his feet. 'I've thought a lot about this problem, father,' he said. 'Now *I* suggest that we gather all our soldiers together here in the city and lay in a good store of food. Then the enemy troops can burn the countryside as much as they like, while we work out a plan of action and attack them when they're not expecting it!'

King Dodon liked this idea—especially the part about laying in a store of food. 'Excellent!' he said. 'I always knew you were clever, my son.'

The nobles nodded in agreement. They always found it safer to agree with the King. But one man, peppery old General Polkan, shouted: 'Stuff and nonsense! I never heard such rubbish in my life. Why—the enemy could lay siege to the city, scale the walls, and take King Dodon himself prisoner before we knew where we were!'

The noblemen thought there was sound sense in this. But when the King remarked irritably that *some* people were too clever for words, they quickly decided to agree with him!

Dodon then asked his second son if he could suggest a solution. The younger Prince stood up. 'My supposedly intelligent elder brother is a dunce!' he said. '*I* think we ought to disband our army at once. The enemy will think we are completely harmless. Then, when *they* have stopped being on their guard, we can reassemble the armies and fall on them suddenly. We'd be bound to win!'

Dodon thought this too was a splendid plan. 'I'm lucky to have two such clever sons,' he said. And of course the nobles agreed. But again General Polkan jumped up impatiently. 'Suppose the enemy refuse to play the game as usual,' he shouted. 'Suppose they attack us first? What would happen then? We should be wiped out—just like that!'

At this King Dodon lost his temper (which was never very steady). He threw a bundle of state papers at the General's head.

'How dare you find fault with my sons' plans?' he yelled. '*Will* you keep quiet, you obstinate old man!'

The courtiers too started throwing things at General Polkan, and there was a great deal of noise and commotion. At last Dodon fell back in his seat, puffing and blowing. 'Well, quarrelling will get us nowhere,' he panted. 'And the real problem is: *how can we tell where the enemy is going to attack next?*'

Obstinate General Polkan

The nobles sat down again, leaving General Polkan doing his best to tidy himself. But no one made any sensible suggestions whatsoever. King Dodon sat brooding dejectedly, his chin on his hand. His crown was all tilted to one side as a result of his throwing things at General Polkan.

Suddenly a tall old man appeared at the top of the staircase, between the sleeping guards. He had strange, piercing blue eyes, and he wore a blue robe embroidered with gold stars and a tall, white, pointed hat. Under one arm he carried a brightly-

coloured bag. The quarrelling courtiers fell silent as
he walked slowly up to the King.

'Greetings, King Dodon,' said the stranger; 'I
used to be chief adviser to your father many years
ago. Now I have come to offer my services to you.'
'That's most kind of you, I'm sure,' King Dodon
replied nervously, not knowing what to make of
this odd-looking stranger.

'I am an astrologer,' continued the old man. 'In
this bag there is a Golden Cockerel, which I have
brought as a gift for Your Majesty. Place it in
some very high position, where it has a good view
over all the countryside round your city. If everything is quiet and secure it will be silent—or it
might sing you a lullaby. But the moment there is
any danger from an enemy attack it will crow loud
enough to wake the dead, so that you will have
plenty of warning and can prepare your armies.'

'Will it really do that? How wonderful!' cried
King Dodon. 'Show me this marvellous bird.'

☆ 20 ☆

The astrologer opened the bag and lifted out a little cockerel that seemed to be made of pure gold. At once it flapped its wings and crowed musically. 'Cock-a-doodle-do!' it sang. 'Sleep in peace and comfort, do-o!'

'What a miracle! Who ever would have believed it!' cried the nobles as they crowded round. King Dodon, of course, was delighted. At last, he thought, he need never worry again about the safety of his kingdom. He ordered servants to place the bird on the palace roof on the point of a long lance. From there it would see the rolling steppes for many miles around.

'How can I possibly reward you enough for bringing me such a wonderful gift?' he said to the old man. 'Ask anything you like in payment, and I will give it to you.'

The astrologer was not interested in the usual kinds of reward, he said. Money and rich jewels only caused trouble. 'But it is kind of you to promise me anything I ask,' he went on; 'if I can have this promise in writing, signed and sealed in the proper manner, I shall be content.'

King Dodon was amazed, and really rather offended. Nobody had ever doubted his word before. 'In this country a promise from me is as good as the law,' he said. 'In fact, it *is* the law! You will have to trust me.'

The astrologer bowed low and quietly left the hall. He walked past the sentries, who were still asleep, down the stair-case and out into the city. Soon he had disappeared among the narrow streets.

From high above the palace the Cockerel crowed again. 'Cock-a-doodle-do! Sleep in peace and comfort, do-o!' it cried. This was just what King Dodon liked to hear. He dismissed his sons and the chattering nobles, and sent for his housekeeper,

Amelfa. When she came, she was followed by servants carrying a carved ivory bed covered with fur rugs, which they placed in the centre of the hall. Dodon yawned and stretched his arms in the sunshine. '*Now* I shall be able to rule the country from my bed if I choose,' he said, sitting down; 'and go hunting, and give parties, and eat as much as I like at dinner. And I need *never* worry about my enemies again!'

'What would you like to eat before you go to sleep, dearie?' asked Amelfa; 'here are some nuts dipped in honey, and some almond biscuits I made specially for you.' 'I'll try the lot!' said the King greedily, and he ate eleven biscuits and lots of nuts before he lay down for his siesta. A sentry called in a drowsy voice, and Amelfa sat fanning the flies away from Dodon's face. He slept like a child, and soon Amelfa too leaned her head on the fur coverlet and fell asleep. Nothing moved in the sunlit hall.

☆ ☆ ☆

Suddenly the Cockerel screamed out in quite a different voice. Everyone woke with a start—except King Dodon. 'Cock-a-doodle-do!' it crowed. 'Danger threatens, wake up, do-o!' Trumpets sounded in the palace, and people ran out of their houses in alarm. But King Dodon slept peacefully on. At last General Polkan came rushing into the council-chamber. 'Sire, sire!' he cried, 'wake up, we shall all be killed!' 'What's the matter?' asked the King drowsily. 'We are being attacked,' cried Polkan; 'the Cockerel is screeching and flapping like a mad thing. The town's in an uproar!'

Dodon sat up and rubbed his eyes. He listened to the excited cry of the Cockerel, and it dawned on him that he would *have* to get up and organize the defence of his city. Grumpily he gave orders for the troops to prepare for battle. Then, watching the crowd of people that had gathered in front of the palace, it occurred to him that this was a good moment to raise some money to pay for the war. So he quickly decreed that they must all pay an extra tax. This made the King feel much happier.

The two Princes came hurrying in. They were not so eager to fight for their country as they ought to have been. 'We are

Screeching and flapping like a mad thing

too young, father,' said the eldest; 'wouldn't it be better if we stayed behind to guard the city treasure?' But the King would not hear of this. 'You must lead the army,' he shouted. 'Take half each, don't quarrel, and mind you come back victorious!' So the two sulky young men marched unwillingly away at the head of their soldiers.

As soon as they were out of sight Dodon went back to bed.

He quickly fell asleep again, and was soon dreaming as pleasantly as before. But, as before, he was not allowed to enjoy it for long. Once more the Cockerel began flapping its wings and screaming: 'Cock-a-doodle-do! Dreadful danger threatens you!' Again trumpets sounded, people ran into the streets, and General Polkan hurried in shouting: 'Wake up! Wake up, King Dodon! Can't you hear the Cockerel?'

'What's the matter now? Why can't you leave me in peace?' roared Dodon, jumping out of bed in a rage.

'They're here again! Another enemy army's invading us, and we've hardly any soldiers left to fight them with!' cried the General. And the Cockerel went on crowing: 'Dreadful danger, wake up, do-o-o!'

Dodon glared up at the excited bird as if he were to blame for all this. 'Well, there's no help for it,' he said at last. 'I shall have to lead an army out myself. Bring me my armour.' But as he had not worn it for so long, his armour was rusty and his shield had got holes in it. 'What a nuisance!' said Dodon; 'everything ought to have been oiled before it was put away, to keep it bright!' The armour was a very tight fit, too, for the King had been putting on weight. However, his attendants managed it. The next thing was to get him on to his horse!

'I do hope he's nice and quiet,' King Dodon said uneasily as a great white charger was led to the foot of the palace steps. 'Quiet as a lamb, sire,' said the groom. But all the same it took three men to heave the King up on to the saddle!

'Now, dearie,' fussed Amelfa, 'you're surely not thinking of going off to fight without any dinner?' 'Oh, I'll have a bite on the way,' said the King. 'I hope we're taking plenty of provisions with us!'

The Cockerel crowed again; King Dodon, the General, and what was left of the army, rode away through the cheering crowds.

King Dodon safely on his horse

☆   ☆   ☆

It is not surprising that this remnant of an army was defeated by the enemy in its very first battle. But an even worse misfortune was in store for the old King. Retreating after the battle on a cold, grey, misty morning, he, General Polkan and their few remaining soldiers came on the bodies of his two sons.

Dodon threw himself on the ground beside them. 'Oh, my dear, good, clever boys,' he wailed. 'What shall I do without them?' Even Polkan almost wept in sympathy.

At that moment the mist began to lift, and they beheld a magnificent tent. Its walls were made of rich brocade that glittered in the rising sun, and from each of its four corners

☆ 25 ☆

3

long pennants fluttered in the breeze. Dodon thought it must be the enemy general's tent and ordered his soldiers to fire a cannon-ball through it. They rushed up a gun, but before they could fire it, a beautiful young woman stepped out of the tent. She took no notice of any of them, but turned towards the sun and sang a lovely song in praise of its warm rays.

'Beautiful lady—who are you?' the King asked nervously. The girl looked at him with mysterious dark eyes.

'I am the Queen of Shemakha,' she replied. She clapped her hands and a slave came out of the tent carrying wine in a silver cup, which she offered to King Dodon. Not being sure if she was a friend or an enemy, he only sipped a little wine, in case it was poisoned. Next, the Queen's slaves spread an embroidered carpet on the ground and placed three cushions on it. King Dodon, General Polkan, and the Queen of Shemakha sat down, and the General tried to make polite conversation.

'Did you have a good night?' he asked the strange girl.

'Not very good,' she answered, 'I woke up before dawn thinking I heard someone speak to me. Then I tried to imagine what sort of man I shall marry, and where I shall find him.'

'Oh, he'll come along some day, don't you worry!' said Polkan.

'Send him away,' demanded the Queen, turning to Dodon: 'I don't like him!'

'Get away, old man,' said the King to Polkan. 'Don't you see you're annoying the lady?'

The Queen drew her cushion closer to Dodon's .'Now I will sing to you,' she said; and she sang a curious song while her slaves accompanied her on their pipes and guitars. Then she persuaded King Dodon to sing her one of his own songs. He did

not want to try at first, saying: 'But it's ages since I did anything of that sort!' The Queen insisted, though, so he tried
strumming on a guitar while he croaked an old ballad he
remembered from his childhood. The Queen laughed heartily.
'Splendid!' she cried.

Next she asked him to dance with her. 'Oh no, really, I'm
much too old and fat!' protested Dodon. 'And my armour's
too heavy.' So the Queen of Shemakha helped him take off his
armour and helmet, and tied a silk scarf round his head like a
turban. She began to dance, tapping the rhythm on a tam-
bourine as she moved gracefully round him. Dodon hopped and

skipped as well as he could, and she laughed
so much at his antics that the tears streamed down her face.

By this time the old King had fallen head over heels in love with the beautiful girl. He had quite forgotten that she might be an enemy of his country. He asked her if she would marry him. 'I am rich,' he pleaded, 'and you shall listen to music all day long, and sleep on a bed filled with rose petals.'

The Queen of Shemakha at once agreed to marry him, and insisted on setting out for his city without delay. Her slaves quickly rolled up the tent, carpet and cushions. The King's soldiers brought up his chariot; he and the Queen climbed into it, and off they drove. General Polkan followed with the soldiers. The Queen of Shemakha's slaves came last, grumbling to each other about their mistress's elderly bridegroom.

As soon as the news reached the city, people came pouring out into the streets to welcome the King home. No one knew who the new Queen was, but they thought she must be a friend because the Cockerel had crowed no more warnings. Amelfa, the royal housekeeper, came out on to the palace steps. She told the people that King Dodon had rescued a beautiful young queen from a dangerous dragon, and that she was going to marry him out of love and gratitude. Unfortunately, she added, the two Princes would not be at their father's wedding as they had met with a misfortune in battle. The people were puzzled, but there was no time to ask any questions.

The procession came in sight, led by the weirdest creatures imaginable, dressed in fantastic clothes. They were followers of the Queen of Shemakha who had joined her somewhere on the way to the city. There were men with the heads of animals, and animals with the heads of men: men with horns and tails and fur on their bodies; dwarfs and giants. King Dodon's citizens had never seen anything like it before!

The King and his bride were seated side by side in his chariot. Dodon looked old and careworn, while the Queen seemed bored; but the people were so delighted with the procession that they did not notice this. They cheered lustily and waved their hats in the air.

Just as the chariot reached the palace steps someone came pushing his way through the crowd. It was the astrologer!

The Queen of Shemakha gave a start. 'Who is that?' she asked abruptly, seizing King Dodon's arm and pointing to the stranger. But the King was delighted to see the old man who had given him the wonderful Cockerel. 'Welcome!' he called out; 'have you come to celebrate my wedding?'

The astrologer answered gravely: 'Great King, I have come to ask for my reward. You gave me your word that I should have anything I wanted in return for the Golden Cockerel.' 'Yes, yes!' said Dodon. 'And what is it you want?'

'The Queen of Shemakha!' replied the astrologer.

Dodon stared at him in astonishment 'You must be mad!' he said. 'I meant—anything within reason! You cannot expect me to give you my own bride! You can have half my kingdom! Surely *that's* enough?'

But the astrologer merely shook his head. 'I have decided to get married,' he replied, 'and I think the Queen of Shemakha will make me a very good wife. I want her and nothing else.'

King Dodon began to grow angry. 'I have never heard such impudence in my life,' he spluttered. 'If you don't go away at once I'll—I'll have you arrested and thrown into a dungeon. GUARDS!' he shouted. Two soldiers quickly seized the astrologer. He struggled and protested: 'But you promised to give me whatever I asked for! What dreadful ingratitude!'

This was too much for Dodon. He seized his gold sceptre and struck the astrologer a heavy blow on the head. The superstitious townspeople shuddered with horror—and the stranger fell dead to the ground.

What a misfortune for a wedding day! Even the skies seemed to be angry, for dark clouds hid the sun and there was a distant roll of thunder. Only the Queen of Shemakha was not at all frightened; she threw back her head and laughed shrilly.

'I didn't mean to kill him!' King Dodon stammered in dismay. 'Nonsense!' laughed the Queen. 'He deserved it for his insolence.' But Dodon shook his head uneasily as he helped her to climb down from the chariot.

They were just starting up the palace steps when the voice of the Golden Cockerel pierced the hush. 'Cock-a-doodle-do-o!' it crowed. 'Cock-a-doodle-do! Now I'll do the same to you!'

And with that the Cockerel soared down from its high lance-tip and drove its sharp beak right into King Dodon's head.

The King fell dead at the foot of the steps, close to where the astrologer lay. It was now almost as dark as night. The

'Now I'll do the same to you!'

people huddled together in terror. And from out of the blackness, the Queen of Shemakha's cruel laughter rang out again and again.

Then the clouds began to move away once more and the sun shone brightly. But the Queen was nowhere to be seen! The astrologer's body, too, had disappeared. So had the Golden Cockerel. General Polkan, Amelfa, and all the soldiers and nobles searched the palace and the city for many days—but they never saw any of them again.

And from that day to this, nobody has been able to discover where the astrologer came from, or where the Queen of Shemakha's country was, or who they really were.

☆ *31* ☆

THE MUSIC

The Russian poet Pushkin (who wrote *Ruslan and Ludmilla*) was told the story of the Golden Cockerel by his nurse when he was a boy. Later he turned it into a poem, and the composer, Rimsky-Korsakov (1844-1908), used the story for his opera.

Rimsky-Korsakov wrote several operas based on fairy tales and legends. *The Golden Cockerel* appeared in 1908, the last year of his life. In this opera he used Russian folk-tunes for the ordinary human beings, while to the Astrologer and the Queen of Shemakha he gave music with an Eastern colouring, expressed in exotic, winding melodies, and strange intervals. This points the contrast in character between the two groups of people: the straightforward, down-to-earth (and sometimes stupid) mortals, and the mysterious supernatural beings.

The main characters each have their own tunes. The Cockerel's call is the most obvious one:

Then there is the Queen of Shemakha's oriental-sounding music:

and the curious tinkling theme that represents the Astrologer:

These three themes are heard in the introduction to the opera, and throughout the work they are always there in some form whenever their particular character is present, or about to appear, or even being spoken of.

King Dodon has several tunes which combine into an exciting march. This is played several times: when the two princes go to repel the invaders; when the King leads out the rest of his army; on the battlefield; and as the wedding procession approaches the palace. The Queen of Shemakha and her attendants have a less warlike march; this accompanies the King and Queen setting out together for his city. There is also a haunting melody—like a lullaby—played by the cellos when King Dodon lies down to sleep in his palace; with flutes and oboes repeating a variation of the Cockerel's soothing theme.

All these themes are included in the orchestral suite of pieces from the opera. This is frequently played at concerts. Perhaps the best-known music in the opera is the Queen's 'Hymn to the Sun,' which is often performed on its own.

The Golden Cockerel has also been made into a ballet.

THE LOVE
FOR THREE ORANGES

THE King of Clubs had a son. He was his only son—and he was very, very ill. So the King summoned all the best doctors in the land to examine him. When they had finished with the Prince they went and talked to his father. But the King got very cross with their long words. 'What is wrong with my son?' he cried. 'Can you cure him?'

'It's quite simple,' the learned doctors replied. 'The Prince has headaches. He can't eat. He can't sleep. He coughs all the time; he has palpitations and fainting fits. In short—it's hopeless. He is suffering from *melancholia*. There *is* no cure for melancholia.'

'Well, if you can't cure him you are no use to me,' said the King angrily. 'Go away, all of you!'

When the doctors had gone, he turned to his friend Pantaloon. 'My poor son!' he wept. 'I'm getting old. If he dies there will only be my niece Princess Clarissa to rule the kingdom, and she's such a strange girl I don't understand her at all. In fact I'm rather frightened of her.'

Pantaloon tried to comfort him. 'Don't cry, sire,' he urged. 'It's undignified for a man in your position.'

The King blew his nose and did his best to look dignified. 'Somebody once said the only thing that would cure the Prince was a good laugh,' he sniffed.

'Then why don't we make him laugh?' cried Pantaloon.

'It's impossible,' said the King; 'nothing can make a person laugh when they have melancholia.'

'But we haven't tried!' protested Pantaloon. 'Let's cheer the whole Court up. We'll have circuses and processions and fancy-dress balls. I'll get Truffaldino to arrange something at once!'

Pantaloon went to the door and shouted at the top of his voice, 'Truf-fal-di-no!' A young man came running in at once. 'Yes, yes, yes? What is it, what is it?' he asked breathlessly.

'Truffaldino,' said the King, 'I want you to arrange some festivities to amuse the Prince. We *must* try to make him laugh, it's the only cure. . . .'

'Festivities!' cried Truffaldino. 'Certainly, sire. I'll see to it. Parties, dancing, acrobats—wonderful stuff.' And off he ran still talking.

'He might have waited to hear the rest of my instructions,' complained the King. Pantaloon chuckled. 'He knows exactly what you want,' he said.

An elderly man entered the room, and immediately Pantaloon frowned. 'Here's the Prime Minister,' he muttered in the King's ear; 'I don't trust him. His eyes are shifty.'

'Oh, I think he's all right,' the King whispered back. 'Ah,

Prime Minister, we're going to have some entertainments. We'll try to cure my son by making him laugh—clowns, conjurers, that sort of thing.'

'But that's not the right way to go about it,' protested the Prime Minister. 'You'll never cure the Prince that way!'

'How do you know?' said the King crossly. 'At least it's worth trying.' And he stalked out of the room.

'Traitor!' growled Pantaloon as he followed the King. 'Donkey!' retorted the Prime Minister.

'What's the matter?' asked a bad-tempered-looking girl who had just come in by another door. This was Princess Clarissa, the King's niece. Not waiting for the Prime Minister to answer, she went on. 'Well, and how is our *dear* cousin, the Prince? Remember what I told you: if he dies and I become Crown Princess, you shall be my husband.'

The Prime Minister bowed. 'Yes, indeed, Princess,' he said.

'Well—what are you doing about it?' asked Clarissa.

'I am doing everything I can to give him nightmares, so that he'll sleep badly and get more and more melancholy,' said the Prime Minister.

'That's much too slow,' objected Clarissa. 'What he needs is a dose of poison or a bullet!'

Just then Truffaldino came running past the open door. 'What is *he* up to?' asked the Princess.

'He's been told to arrange an entertainment, to see if it will make the Prince laugh,' explained the Prime Minister.

'Make him laugh!' exclaimed Clarissa angrily. 'Why, you know very well that if once he laughs he'll be cured! You see what comes of your slow way of doing things!'

At that moment a vase fell with a crash from a nearby table.

The Prime Minister was nearly startled out of his wits. 'What was that?' he cried. He kicked the table over. Underneath crouched a Negro servant-girl. 'Aha!' cried the Prime Minister. 'You've been spying and eavesdropping, have you? And listening to government secrets? I'll have you beheaded, my girl!'

The Prime Minister was nearly startled out of his wits

'But I'm on your side!' protested the black girl. 'I can help you. And there's someone much cleverer than me who wants to help you, too. That's Fata Morgana!'

Clarissa and the Prime Minister knew that Fata Morgana was a powerful fairy, and were delighted to hear that she was their friend. 'Very well,' said the Prime Minister. 'We'll let you off this time.' And the three of them went away together, whispering dark secrets.

☆   ☆   ☆

Up in his bedroom, the Prince lay huddled in an armchair, dressed in a warm gown and wearing a night-cap. On a table beside him stood all sorts of medicine bottles and jars of ointment. He was in the depths of despair.

Truffaldino came running in. He tried to cheer the Prince up by doing a comic dance, but the Prince only moaned. 'Stop—stop! My head is aching, and my back hurts, and I've pains in my knees, *and* the earache!'

Truffaldino stopped dancing. 'Your Highness,' he panted, 'there's going to be a pageant, specially for you, in the great hall, so we must dress you in your best clothes and take you down to see it.' 'Oh no, no!' cried the Prince. 'I couldn't possibly go, it would be the death of me!' 'But it will be enormous fun!' pleaded Truffaldino. 'Listen, Highness: it's starting already!' The band had struck up a lively march and he was longing to be downstairs.

But the Prince did not seem to hear the music. 'I want my medicine!' he sobbed.

'Medicine's no good to you!' snapped Truffaldino. 'You'll poison yourself if you go on swallowing all that muck!' And he swept up the bottles and jars and threw them all out of the window!

The Prince burst into tears again. Truffaldino took no notice. He wrapped his Highness in a fur cloak, lifted him up on to his shoulder, and marched downstairs with him.

In the great hall all the courtiers were assembled, waiting for the entertainment to begin. Truffaldino put the Prince into the chair beside the King and tucked the fur cloak round him. Then he made the King a deep bow and ordered the doors at the end of the hall to be opened. 'Item number one!' he

announced proudly.

A host of clowns and acrobats came rushing in, carrying large clubs and sticks. They proceeded to fight a mock battle in the centre of the hall, and in the end half of them pretended to be killed.

The courtiers clapped heartily, but the Prince only complained about the noise. 'It's made my headache worse,' he whimpered. 'And this hall's full of draughts, too.'

So Truffaldino sent the funny men away and ran about busily preparing for the next item. It was then that the Prime Minister noticed a shabby old woman among the courtiers.

'Who are you, old hag?' he asked indignantly. 'You've no right to be here. Suppose the King were to see you!'

'Sh—sh—I am Fata Morgana!' the old

woman whispered; 'as long as I'm here, *nothing* can make the Prince laugh.'

'Ah, I understand!' gloated the Prime Minister, looking round cautiously to make sure nobody else had noticed her.

Truffaldino clapped his hands and announced, 'Item number two!' A fountain of wine began to play in the middle of the hall. 'It's the very best wine,' Truffaldino boasted. The clowns rushed into the hall again, carrying all sorts of jars which they tried to fill with the wine. But the jets rose and fell, playing now on this side of the fountain, now on the other. It was very difficult to catch any of the wine, and the clowns got very wet. They squabbled, and pushed, and tripped over one another, and a great many jars got broken, and much wine was spilled.

The courtiers found this irresistibly funny. 'Surely *that* made the Prince laugh?' asked Truffaldino, mopping his eyes. 'No, it didn't!', replied the King gloomily. As for the Prince, he just wailed, 'I want to go back to bed!'

Truffaldino was hurt. 'It's no use! Nothing on earth will make the Prince laugh!' He turned away in disgust, just as old Fata Morgana, the wicked fairy, started to cross the hall. 'Now what are *you* doing here? asked Truffaldino crossly. 'Get along out, old woman.' 'Don't speak to me like that, young man, I've a perfect right to be here,' she squeaked. 'Nonsense!' snapped Truffaldino, 'this is no place for anyone as shabby as you. How you got in I can't imagine, but you're going out this instant.' 'Leave me alone,' screeched the old woman. 'Well,' said Truffaldino, 'if you won't go by yourself I shall have to help you!' He gave her a push. 'Ow!' she squealed indignantly, tripped over a wine-jar, and fell down with a bump.

Immediately there was a sound that made everybody stare in astonishment: the Prince was laughing! 'Ha, ha!' he chuckled, quite quietly at first. 'He he he he! Ho ho ho ho ho!' He laughed louder and louder, holding his sides and wiping his eyes. 'Oh, what a funny old woman!' he gasped, 'when she sat down—bump!—like that—it was the funniest thing—I've ever seen! Ha ha ha ha ha!'

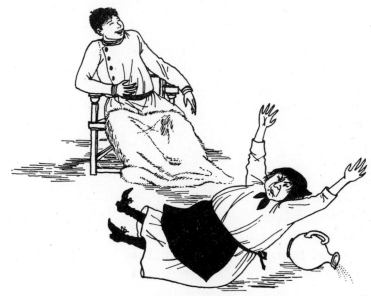

The Prince was laughing!

The King of Clubs, Pantaloon, Truffaldino and all the courtiers could hardly believe their ears. 'Why, he's *laughing!*' they said. Then they began to laugh, too, until the whole court was rocking with laughter. Truffaldino seized Pantaloon and waltzed him round the great hall. The King danced a sort of jig in his chair of state. Only Princess Clarissa and the Prime Minister sat apart, looking absolutely furious.

Fata Morgana picked herself up slowly, with a horrible expression on her face. 'You villain!' she cried, turning fiercely on the Prince. 'How dare you laugh at me? I'll put a curse on you. You shall fall in love with three oranges—three oranges, I tell you. You shall love them so much that you will have to go and search for them far and wide. You will leave your father's palace and go and look for them!—At once!'

The evil old fairy turned and made her way out of the hall. There was a howling noise, and a whole army of little imps appeared and danced round her as she vanished.

The spell worked quickly. The Prince began to walk restlessly up and down. 'Three oranges!' he repeated over and over again. 'I love three oranges!' He ran about the hall as if he had lost something. Truffaldino and Pantaloon managed to catch him but he struggled to escape from them. 'Let me go! I must find my three oranges!' he cried. 'But you don't know where to look!' said Pantaloon. 'Yes, I do,' said the Prince. 'They're in the witch's castle leagues away in the great desert. I must go there at once! Bring me my boots and my sword! Truffaldino, you must come with me!' There was certainly no sign left of his Highness's melancholia!

But the King was appalled at the idea of his only son travelling about the world on such a mad adventure—especially to a witch's castle. 'I absolutely *forbid* you to go, my son,' he said. 'You are my heir, and the kingdom is more important than your three oranges.'

The Prince merely pulled on his boots and buckled on his

sword. 'I must go, father,' he said; 'and if I stayed here I should certainly catch melancholia again!' This frightened the King even more. 'In that case you'd better go,' he agreed hurriedly. 'But do take care! Look after him, Truffaldino!'

So the Prince and Truffaldino set out. The moment they were outside the palace gate a strong wind blew them right off the ground. Away they flew over meadows, mountains and lakes, towards the desert where the witch's castle lay. Although they did not know it, this wind was a devil who was jealous of Fata Morgana, blowing them along with a pair of magic bellows.

When they got near the castle he stopped blowing and they fell to the ground, rolling over and over in the sand.

'That was a very powerful wind,' said the

Prince as they picked themselves up. 'But it seems to have brought us to the right place: I feel it in my bones.'

And there, over the brow of a hill, stood the witch's castle. A dreadful-looking place it was, with grim walls and a huge iron gate. Luckily this had been left ajar, and the Prince and Truffaldino just managed to squeeze through.

They found themselves in a dirty court-yard full of barrels and boxes. Clouds of steam came puffing out of an open door, and a gruff voice was singing. Truffaldino began to tremble. 'Oh what a horrible place,' he whispered. 'I'm frightened!'

'I'm frightened too,' said the Prince. 'But I *must* find those three oranges. They're sure to be in the kitchen—over there where the steam is coming from.'

'Don't go in, your Highness,' pleaded Truffaldino. 'Don't you hear that dreadful voice?'

But the Prince was quite determined. Then, just as he got to the kitchen door, there was an ear-splitting crash inside. As quick as a flash the two young men hid behind the piles of barrels. A gigantic woman in a white cap and apron came out of the door, holding a great soup ladle in her hand.

'Who's there?' she called. 'Someone was talking; who is it?'

She started searching the court-yard, shouting all the time: 'You'd better come out! Nobody can hide from me for long!' And sure enough she found Truffaldino trying to squeeze himself into a tiny space behind a barrel.

The cook seized him by the ear. 'Now who is this little man, I wonder?' she cried. 'Shall I throw him into the fire?' 'Oh no, no, please don't do that!' wailed Truffaldino. 'Well, then, shall I bash him with my little spoon?' suggested the cook, flourishing the enormous ladle. But fortunately she noticed a bit of blue ribbon he was wearing on his jacket. 'What have you got there?' she asked. 'A p-p-piece of ribbon,' stammered Truffaldino, half dead with fright. 'It's a very pretty colour,' said the cook. 'Wouldn't you like to give it to me, as a souvenir?'

Out of the corner of his eye, Truffaldino saw the Prince creep past them and into the kitchen. 'Would you like my ribbon *very* much?' asked Truffaldino, teasing the huge cook to gain time. 'More than anything else in the world,' she said. 'Very well, then,' said Truffaldino, pretending to be extremely generous. 'You shall have it.' And he untied the ribbon and gave it to her.

The cook took it in her great hands. 'Oh, what a beautiful piece of ribbon,' she crooned; 'just the colour of my eyes!'

Truffaldino tiptoed into the kitchen. And there was the Prince, carefully holding three fine oranges!

'Quick!' said Truffaldino, and whipped them into his knapsack. They crept back past the cook, who had tied the ribbon in her hair and was admiring her reflection in the soup ladle. So they took to their heels and ran away from the grim castle as fast as they could.

When they had gone some way towards home, Truffaldino began to complain how heavy the oranges were. And indeed they were growing larger all the time! He and the Prince had to carry them in their arms. But the oranges went on growing until they were too big to be held at all. So the young men put them on the ground and rolled them along.

'I've never seen oranges like *this* before,' Truffaldino panted; 'they're as big as if they had human beings inside them!'

At last they were too exhausted to go further. 'I'm quite

worn out,' gasped the Prince. 'I must lie down and have a nap.'
He curled himself up in the shadow of a rock and was fast
asleep in a moment.

They crept back past the cook

'He's lucky,' grumbled Truffaldino to himself. 'I'm much
too thirsty to sleep, and there's not a drop of water anywhere.
I shall die of thirst, and in a hundred years' time they'll find
my bones all whitened by the sun, like a camel's. Oh dear!
I must have a drink!' He stared at the enormous oranges. 'How
juicy they look,' he thought; 'just *one* of them would save our
lives!'

☆ 46 ☆

Truffaldino took his sword and cut open one of the oranges. But instead of juice he found a pale, pretty girl inside it, dressed in white.

'Please give me a drink of water,' she sobbed; 'I'm dying of thirst!'

Truffaldino felt desperately sorry for her. 'Wait,' he cried, and cut the second orange into two neat halves.

To his horror, a girl in white stepped out of this one too! 'I'm *so* thirsty,' she cried; 'please give me a drink of water or I shall die!' Truffaldino was now thoroughly frightened. 'There isn't any water,' he wept. 'Oh whatever shall I do?'

'Help me, help me, or I shall die,' gasped the first girl. 'Water, please—water!' sighed the second. Their voices grew weaker and weaker; they sank down and lay motionless on the hot sand. Truffaldino, panic-stricken, had only one thought: to escape before the Prince woke up and discovered what he had done. So he ran away faster than he had ever run before.

At last the Prince woke up. 'Truffaldino, where are you?' he called. Then he sat up and saw the two girls and the orange halves. 'Heavens!' he cried, jumping to his feet. 'These girls must have been inside the oranges. Yes, *now* I know who is in the third one: a princess—for me!' He drew his sword and carefully cut the last orange in two. A third girl in white stepped out, more beautiful than either of the others.

'I am Princess Ninetta, daughter of the King of the Antipodes,' she said. 'I have been waiting for you a very long time.' 'My beloved Princess,' said the Prince, 'I have been searching for you through the whole wide world.'

'Please give me a drink of water,' begged Princess Ninetta; 'I am dying of thirst!' The Prince was more sensible than

The Princess seized it gratefully

Truffaldino. He quickly climbed to the top of the rock, and there on the other side of it he saw a tiny lake. He ran round to it, took off one of his boots, and filled it with water. He carried it back to Ninetta and the princess seized it gratefully. 'You have saved my life,' she said when she had had a good drink. 'You must be the kindest man in the world.' 'And you are certainly the most beautiful princess,' replied the Prince; 'from now on you shall drink from gold and crystal vessels. But we must go and meet my father and his court. His palace isn't far from here.'

'I cannot meet your father in these dirty old clothes!' said Ninetta. 'I haven't had a new dress since I was shut up in the orange by that terrible witch's cook. I'm so shabby your father would never believe I was really a princess. Would you go on and warn him, and bring me back a new dress to put on?'

'Yes, Princess,' said the Prince, 'wait for me by this rock.'

He hurried off, so happy that his feet seemed to have wings. And Ninetta settled herself comfortably on the rock to wait for him.

Now Fata Morgana, the wicked fairy, was furious. She came creeping up to Ninetta's rock and muttered a spell which turned the poor Princess into a rat. The rat ran down the rock and disappeared, and instead there sat the ragged black girl whom Clarissa and the Prime Minister had found under the table.

'Good!' said Fata Morgana, 'you must say *you* are Princess Ninetta, and the King will be angry with his son and throw him into prison, and everything will turn out as I planned after all.'

Soon the Prince returned, bringing his father and a crowd of courtiers with him. They were full of curiosity about the Princess their Prince had found inside an orange. 'There she is,' cried the Prince, seeing a figure in white sitting on the rock. 'This is Princess Ninetta, father!' But when the girl turned round and he saw her black face he was horrified. 'Oh no—*that's* not Ninetta!' he cried. The black girl began to sob. 'How can you be so cruel? You *promised* to marry me, here by this very rock. And there is the orange you rescued me from.'

The King of Clubs looked grave. 'Princes must never break their word,' he said. 'If you promised to marry this lady, then you must do so at once. Give her your hand, and we will go back to the palace and arrange the ceremony.'

The Prince was puzzled and desperately unhappy, but the King would not listen to his protests. So he was forced to take the black girl by the hand, and they all made their way back to the palace. Clarissa and the Prime Minister were gloating in the rear: they felt sure the Prince would soon get melancholia again—now that he had lost Ninetta.

Preparations for the wedding began immediately. When everything was ready the courtiers crowded into the hall. The King led the black girl to her seat. But as they came closer they saw a rat sitting on the crimson cushion, washing its whiskers!

The black girl shrieked; instantly the rat disappeared—and there was Ninetta! She looked so beautiful that the King at once knew her to be a real Princess. The Prince was overjoyed, and ran to embrace his bride.

'Who is this black girl?' asked the King sternly. 'I know, I know!' cried an excited voice. Truffaldino rushed in from the kitchen, where he had been supervising the wedding feast. 'If you please, your Majesty, she is a friend of Princess Clarissa's and the Prime Minister. I've seen them all talking!'

'Arrest them at once!' thundered the King, his face scarlet with anger. But the black girl was already speeding down the long hall. Clarissa ran after her, holding up her long skirts, with the Prime Minister just behind. The guards leapt after them and quickly began to gain on the Prime Minister, who was too fat to run fast.

At this moment Fata Morgana appeared, not as an old woman but as herself—a wicked fairy in black and scarlet robes. She struck the floor with her wand and a gaping hole appeared. And into it they all fell as they ran—the black girl, Clarissa, and the fat Prime Minister! Then Fata Morgana jumped after them and a cloud of smoke and flames rose up. When this had cleared away there was no hole, and not the slightest trace of any of them, though the guards searched the entire palace.

'Well, they've gone. Let us hope they never come back,' said the King of Clubs. 'There's nothing to prevent us from enjoying the wedding feast now.'

The courtiers waved their fans and handkerchiefs and cried 'Long live the King!' 'No, you must say "Long live the Prince and Princess",' he replied. So the obedient courtiers shouted, 'Long live the Prince and Princess!'

And the Prince and Ninetta did live long, and were very, very happy.

☆　　☆　　☆

THE MUSIC

The opera called *The Love for Three Oranges* is by Serge Prokofiev. He wrote it in 1919, which is only eleven years later than Rimsky-Korsakov's *Golden Cockerel*. The music of the two operas, however, is very different. While Rimsky-Korsakov was a man of the nineteenth century, Prokofiev belongs to the twentieth; his music is altogether modern in style. He wrote the libretto —the words of the opera—himself. The story comes from a play by Carlo Gozzi, an eighteenth-century Italian playwright.

Unlike *Ruslan and Ludmilla* and *The Golden Cockerel*, each act of *The Love for Three Oranges* runs in one continuous movement. So it is more difficult to play bits from it. But there is one tune that almost everybody knows—the March:

This comes several times in the opera. It first appears when the entertainment to make the Prince laugh is being prepared. That is what Truffaldino hears up in the Prince's bedroom; you will remember how he carries the Prince downstairs, impatient to begin the show. First the march is played by a small band off-stage. At the end of the scene the full orchestra plays it —and very exciting it sounds. Then we hear the march when the Prince brings his father to the rock where he had left Princess Ninetta to wait. And it comes again at full strength as they all march back in procession to the palace for the wedding.

Prokofiev was so fond of this splendid music that he brought it into his *Cinderella* ballet. Sometimes the march is played at concerts by itself. It is also included in a suite for orchestra, selected from the opera. This suite is made up of six pieces altogether. It includes a Scherzo where you can hear the devil's magic bellows blowing Truffaldino and the Prince to the witch's castle; a piece called 'The Prince and Princess'; and finally 'The Escape.' In this the music vividly describes the wicked fairy, Fata Morgana, the black girl, the Prime Minister and Princess Clarissa running away from the King's guards. You may be able to hear them falling down the hole if you listen carefully.

☆　　☆　　☆